WHERE else in the WILD?

MORE Camouflaged Creatures Concealed...and Revealed

WHERE else in the WiLD?

MORE Camouflaged Creatures Concealed...and Revealed

Ear-Tickling Poems by David M. Schwartz and Yael Schy | Eye-Tricking Photos by Dwight Kuhn

TRICYCLE PRESS

BERKELEY | TORONTO

CAN YOU FiND ME?

TURN TO THE LAST PAGE IF YOU'RE STUMPED.

If you were a frog or a fish or a bird or a bug—or almost any other kind of animal— you would probably live longer if you could hide with your colors. Whether you were looking for food or trying to avoid being someone else's food, camouflage could help you survive. If a predator doesn't see you, it can't eat you. If your prey doesn't see you, it can be your next meal.

In our previous book, *Where in the Wild? Camouflaged Creatures Concealed. . .and Revealed*, we introduced ten well-camouflaged animals. We had so much fun with *Where in the Wild?* that we decided to write this sequel. Now you can puzzle over eleven more hidden animals—and we've got some wild ones!

You'll discover an enchanting collection of camouflaged creatures: an insect that looks just like the leaves on which it feeds; a fish with venomous spines you wouldn't want to touch but may find impossible to see; a mammal as white as freshly fallen snow in the winter, but as brown as bare earth in the summer. These animals and others lie in wait to challenge your powers of observation.

Both *Where in the Wild?* and *Where Else in the Wild?* feature photographs of hidden animals lurking in their natural environment. Can you spot them? Poems provide clues about each animal so you can try to figure out what you're looking for. When you're ready to find out who's hiding and where, lift the photo page. The camouflaged creature is revealed in its hiding place. Then, read the fascinating facts on the facing page about this animal's natural history and how it uses camouflage to survive.

This book works the same way as *Where in the Wild?*, but there is a difference: some of these photographs have not just one camouflaged creature, but two or three. Each poem will give you clues about how many animals you're looking for. Before you lift the page, try to find them all. Good luck!

Measure by Measure

creeping and crawling, I bend and extend—smooth, hairless body, legs at each end

green as these tendrils of curlicue vine—standing immobile at danger's first sign

chomping and munching, feeding all day—measure by measure, inching my way

LIFT TO
FIND ME!

Inchworm

Inch by inch, inchworms inch their way along a branch or vine. Also called measuring worms or loopers, inchworms are the larvae of geometer moths. The word geometer means "earth measurer" because the larvae of geometer moths appear to be "measuring" with their inch-long bodies as they move. With legs at each end, they bend into a loop and then straighten out to their full length.

Green, brown, gray, or black, inchworms of many species look like the twigs of the trees they feed upon. The resemblance is so strong that predators have a hard time noticing them. If danger comes too close, the inchworm makes a silken thread from a gland in its mouth and slides down the thread. Hanging in midair, it looks even more like a twig. When the threat has passed, the inchworm climbs back up the thread to munch on leaves once again.

Like most insect larvae, inchworms undergo complete metamorphosis. This process begins when they lower themselves to the ground and burrow into the earth to spin silken cocoons. They pass the winter as pupae until they emerge in the spring, fully transformed into adult moths. After finding a mate, female moths lay eggs. These hatch into larvae and the daily routine of feeding and inching, inching and feeding, begins again.

Praying as I Prey

elegance in white
poised upon an orchid bloom
praying as I prey

LIFT TO
FIND ME!

Orchid Mantis

The orchid mantis is a master of disguise and a marvel of the insect world. Like other praying mantises, the orchid mantis hunts while holding its forelegs together. This is how the praying mantis gets its name, but of course it is not praying at all— it is preying!

To track potential prey, the mantis can rotate its head a full ninety-degrees to either side without moving the rest of its body. When another insect comes close, the mantis's barbed forelegs lash out to nab the victim and hold it tight against the jagged spikes of its muscular legs.

North American mantises are usually green or brown, but the colors of the Malaysian orchid mantis are more striking. They range from pink to yellow to white, allowing the predator to blend with orchids in the rainforests of Malaysia and Indonesia.

So effective is the orchid mantis's amazing camouflage that it doesn't even have to hide inside a flower. It can stand next to one, or on top of a spray of flowers. Visiting insects may confuse the mantis's body with one of the blooms, and fly right to it! Either way, instead of getting its own meal of sweet nectar, the insect becomes a meal for the mantis.

One Great Bound

I'm fast and strong,
my feet are long,
and when I'm on my way,
in one great bound
I leave the ground
then land ten feet away!

When cold winds blow,
I match the snow—
my fur's a soft, white gown.
But then I molt
and change my coat.
By summer I've turned brown!

LIFT TO
FIND ME!

Snowshoe Hare

What can leap ten feet in a single bound? A snowshoe hare! With enormous, padded hind feet and powerful thigh muscles, hares can run more than twenty-five miles per hour and quickly change direction to confuse pursuers. Not only are hares fast, but they have acute hearing that alerts them to an approaching threat so they can make their getaway. Unlike rabbits, which dash into underground warrens, hares try to outrun danger.

During the day, hares rest in bushes or hollow logs. At night, they travel long distances in search of grass, leaves, twigs, and bark to eat. A hare's brown summer coat turns white in winter. By matching the colors of its environment, hares can better hide from predators.

Hares breed quickly—each female can have up to sixteen young each year. Unlike rabbits, born hairless and blind, newborn snowshoe hares have full fur coats. They can see right away, and within minutes of birth, they are hopping around.

The number of snowshoe hares in an area can sometimes skyrocket—and then, even more quickly, crash. In some years, hare populations grow to more than ten thousand animals in a single square mile. In other years, that number plunges to just one. Understanding these dramatic fluctuations is important to scientists, who hope to learn more about what causes animal populations to thrive or fail.

Harbinger

In wintertime, when ponds and rivers freeze,
I hibernate beneath the bark of trees.
When warm days come, I wake and start to sing.
I'm often called a harbinger of spring.

To find a mate, I make a peeping sound
by puffing out my throat until it's round.
I'm known for chirping loudly through the night.
To find me, use your hearing, not your sight!

LIFT TO
FIND ME!

Spring Peeper

How do we know that spring has arrived? Is it the colorful crocuses pushing up through the earth? Or the robin singing in the yard? Or the blossoming fruit trees? Or is it the whistle of a small tree frog? The spring peeper's name comes from its loud mating call, which is one of the earliest signs of spring in many parts of North America.

All amphibians begin life in water. Peeper tadpoles hatch from a clutch of up to one thousand eggs. As they mature, they lose their tails, grow legs, and develop lungs. By late summer, the tadpoles have become frogs. They leave the pond and head to the forest where their sticky toe pads help them climb trees. During the winter, they hibernate under logs or loose bark. A peeper can survive even if most of its body freezes.

As distinctive as its springtime call, the dark "X" across the backs of most spring peepers may confuse the eyes of predators who don't realize they're looking at a frog. With its tiny size (under one and a half inches), nocturnal habits, and skin that can rapidly darken or lighten to match the background, the noisy spring peeper is easy to hear but hard to see.

A male may call up to twenty-five times per minute by inflating a vocal sac under its chin. Often, many males join together in a noisy chorus. If you visit a pond when peepers are singing, you might want to bring earplugs!

Garbage Collectors

We live underwater in creeks and in brooks.
When frightened, we hide under rocks or in nooks.
We swim only backwards (we see where we've been!).
And as we get bigger, we shed our old skin.

Losing a leg is no problem for us.
We just grow a new one without any fuss.
We've got eight little legs, plus two that are jumbo.
Some folks like to eat us—they put us in gumbo.

We scavenge for food. We're garbage collectors.
But don't get too close—we're fearsome protectors.
If fingers or toes come within half an inch,
they're going to suffer a terrible pinch!

LOOK AGAIN! THERE ARE 3 OF US HIDING HERE

Crayfish

Crayfish have many names. These residents of streams, rivers, swamps, and ponds are also called crawdads, crawfish, freshwater lobsters, mudbugs, and sometimes even just plain old "bugs"!

Like crabs and lobsters, crayfish are crustaceans. Their segmented bodies have ten legs—four pairs of small legs used for walking and probing underwater crevices for food, and one pair of large claws, or "pincers," which capture prey and defend against predators. If you're unlucky enough to be pinched by a crayfish, you'll quickly find out how sharp and powerful its pincers can be!

The hard outside skeleton, or "exoskeleton," of a crayfish is thin but tough. It does not expand as the animal inside grows. When the crayfish gets too big for its "armor," it must shed its old exoskeleton and grow a larger one. This is called "molting."

Active at night, crayfish are bottom dwellers who often pass the day under rocks, logs, or sand. Their colors—yellow, tan, green, red, or dark brown—help them disappear. If startled, a crayfish will rapidly flip its tail to swim backwards. A female uses her tail in another important way: to carry and protect her eggs. The young hatch and stay attached to the underside of their mother's tail until they are big enough to swim on their own.

Crayfish are not fussy eaters. They are scavengers who will eat almost anything, including small animals, both living and dead—and even their own molted exoskeletons. Fish, herons, otters, snakes, and even people find crayfish tasty. In Louisiana, they are a very popular dish, often cooked in a spicy stew called gumbo.

Winter's Morn

winter's morn...cold and gray
time to eat...can't delay
feeder hangs...by the door
peck, snap, gulp...seeds galore!

door swings out...human near
what to do? outta here!
land on bush...heartbeat slows
wait it out...till he goes.

now he's gone...coast is clear
back to seeds...no more fear
feast again...safely now
what's that sound?
meow meow meowWWWw!

LIFT TO
FIND ME!

Black-Capped Chickadee

Chickadees arrive and a snow-covered backyard bursts into life. "Chick-a-dee-dee-dee," the small birds call to each other. Like gymnasts, they swing from branch to branch, sometimes hanging upside down. But they're not after medals — they're after food. They scour the bark of trees in search of seeds, insects, and insect eggs. If they're lucky, the yard will have a bird feeder stocked with seeds.

To chickadees, which do not migrate to warmer climates in winter as many birds do, a feeder is an all-you-can-eat feast. When insects are scarce, the feeder's stash of energy-rich seeds can mean the difference between life and death.

Like mammals, birds are warm-blooded. Small birds have a big problem in cold weather: they lose heat so rapidly that they can easily freeze to death.

To stay warm, chickadees fluff up their feathers. The soft, fine feathers found beneath a bird's outer feathers are called "down," and down is one of nature's best insulators. It helps keep body heat inside. Still, the birds must fuel their internal furnaces with food. During the short days of winter, birds are on a frantic mission to get enough food to stay warm and nourished. They feed constantly from sunrise to sunset. For many chickadees, bird feeders provide about one-fourth of the food that they eat.

Always wary of predators (or large upright mammals they mistake for predators), a chickadee doesn't linger at the feeder. At the first sign of danger, it grabs a seed and flies off. With its black, white, and brown feathers, a chickadee finds a perfect hiding spot in a bare winter shrub and quietly waits for the peril to pass.

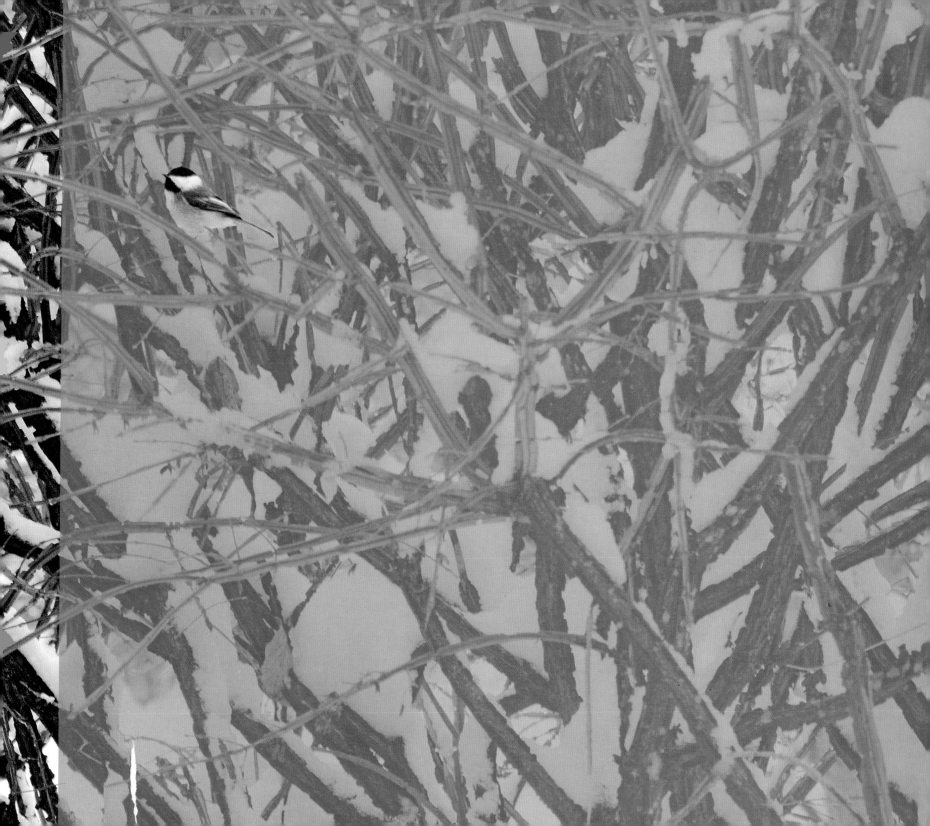

Upside Down

In darkest night I hunt for flies, until the sun begins to rise.

At break of day I'm upside down, holding tight above the ground.

Here I rest the whole day through, upon a stalk of brown bamboo.

LIFT TO
FIND ME!

Lined Leaf-Tailed Gecko

From the rainforests of Madagascar, the world's largest island, come nine species of lizards known as leaf-tailed geckos. They feed at night and spend their days resting, usually head-down on a tree trunk or stalk. To stay alive until the next sunset, they are experts at hiding in plain sight.

These geckos are so good at "disappearing" that the Malagasy people of Madagascar find them spooky. They think the lizards are possessed by evil spirits, and for this reason one species is called the satanic leaf-tailed gecko. Its whole body resembles a curled-up dead leaf.

Some species go even further in their disguise. The mossy leaf-tailed gecko has loose flaps and fringes all over its body. If you were walking among moss- and lichen-covered trees, you'd think it was just part of the landscape. Plastered flat against a tree, it doesn't even cast a shadow in bright light.

Geckos are famous for their ability to run vertically or upsidedown on any surface, even glass. Scientists have found that the pads of geckos' toes are covered with thousands of microscopic hairs, each far thinner than the finest human hair. These hairs divide at the tips into millions of even tinier hairs. The molecules of these ultra-tiny hairs "stick" to the molecules of almost anything.

Q & A

What looks like a leaf, but has wings, legs, and eyes?
An insect that hides with a clever disguise.

How does it manage to fool us like that?
It's totally green and its abdomen's flat.

A remarkable bug! How else is it shrewd?
To resemble a leaf, it appears to be chewed.

But an insect must move—does it amble with ease?
It sways when it walks, like a leaf in the breeze.

Does this really exist? Can you show it to me?
Just look at the picture. Sharp eyes will find three!

LOOK AGAIN! THERE ARE 3 OF US HIDING HERE

Leaf Insect

Some animals look like something they are not—something predators won't attack. Biologists call this "mimicry." One of the most remarkable mimics in the animal kingdom is the leaf insect, which, as its name suggests, looks just like a leaf.

A leaf insect's mimicry doesn't stop with its imitation of a leaf's shape and color. On a leaf insect's wings are ridges that look like the veins of a leaf. Its sides can even have small "chew marks" to make the "leaf" look more authentic. When a leaf insect walks, it sways gently from side to side, like a leaf in a light breeze. Completing the disguise, a leaf insect's eggs actually look like seeds! Some people call leaf insects by another name: "walking leaves."

Leaf insects are part of a larger group of insects known as "stick insects." The best-known stick insects are walking sticks, which mimic twigs.

Leaf insects are native only to parts of Asia and Australia but walking sticks are found in many parts of the world, including North America. Next time you're outside, see if you can find one.

Take a Close Look

There's Mickey and Minnie, as cute as can be,
and three in a song who simply can't see.

There's debonair Stuart who wins with his charm,
and visiting cousins from city and farm.

But strangest of all is a high-tech device.
To make it perform, you click once or click twice.

Forget about them. Take a close look at me.
I'm not in old stories. I'm not on TV.

I don't grab the limelight. I don't wear bright clothes.
I've got whiskers and fur, and a sharp, twitchy nose.

My color's called "mousy"—it helps me survive.
If I keep out of sight, I might stay alive!

LIFT TO
FIND ME!

White Footed Mouse

In the fantasy world of stories, movies, TV, and amusement parks, mice are superstars. But in the real world of grasslands, forests, roadsides, and riverbanks, daily life for a mouse is a struggle to stay nourished and avoid becoming nourishment. Owls, foxes, weasels, and many other sharp-eyed predators hunt mice. Facing many perils each day, few wild mice live beyond the ripe old age of two.

One of the most abundant mammals in North America, white-footed mice live in woodlands across the continent. Nocturnal acrobats, they move deftly from branch to branch and tree to tree, finding their footing even in the dark of night. They raise their young in abandoned bird nests or in burrows beneath the leaf litter. White-footed mice do not hibernate. To get through the winter they store, or "cache," dry food, hiding it in granaries near their nests, using cheek pouches similar to those of squir-rels to transport the food. White-footed mice are known to cache seeds, acorns, and nuts by the quart.

Like many animals sought by predators, white-footed mice are dark above and light below. Think about it: eyes looking upward for tree-dwelling prey will see only the mouse's light underside blending into the sky; eyes looking downward will see its brownish top—hard to notice against the dark ground. The dull, brown fur of a mouse is sometimes described as "mousy." It pays to be mousy if you're a mouse!

Be Cautious!!!

be wary
we're scary
we're ugly
not snuggly
fins pierce
we're fierce
hey enemy
we're venom-y
don't squash us
BE CAUTIOUS!!!

LOOK AGAIN!
THERE ARE 2 OF US HIDING HERE

Scorpionfish

If there were Olympic Games for underwater camouflage, the scorpionfish would take the gold! One of nature's camouflage champions, the scorpionfish is the opposite of what most people expect of a tropical fish. It is not sleek, graceful, or brightly colored. Its color is a mottled mixture of gray, brown, and black. This strange-looking fish blends so well into a reef or rocky ocean bottom that you'd have trouble finding one, even if you knew exactly where to look!

Not seeing a well-camouflaged scorpionfish can be dangerous indeed. You would not want to step on the needlelike spines of its dorsal fin—in some species they can be more than a foot long! Worse yet, the spines work like hypodermic needles, injecting potent venom into an unlucky victim. Pity the poor diver who puts a hand or foot in the wrong place. Like venomous snakes, this fish has a toxin that causes excruciating pain and even paralysis. The only good news is that usually it is not fatal to humans.

Unlike snakes, scorpionfish do not use their poisons to kill prey. They have another way to do that: lying still on the sea floor, a scorpionfish ambushes unsuspecting fish by sucking water into its gaping mouth with great force. Unaware of the hidden predator, many kinds of fish—even moray eels, rays, snappers, and small sharks—can get caught in the deadly current.

Ambushed!

bug

AMBUSH

bug

AMBUSH

bug

AMBUSH

A^{bug}MBUSH

AMBUSH

AMBUSHED!

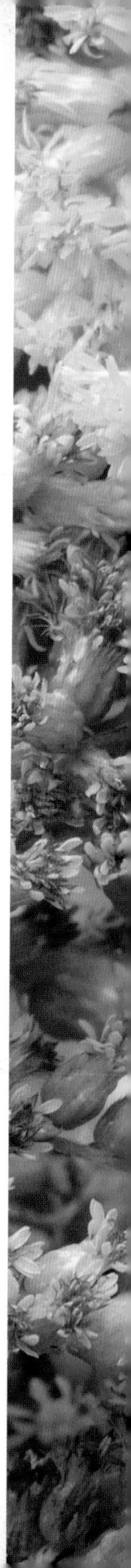

LIFT TO
FIND ME!

Ambush Bug

Bizarre. Pre-historic. Scary-looking. That's the ambush bug, a strange-looking insect that sits on a flower waiting to pounce on passing insects. With enormous, curved forelegs, the ambush bug grabs and lifts the visitor to its needle-sharp mouthparts—ambushed!

People often use the word "bug" to mean any insect. Even entomologists, scientists who study insects, sometimes do this. But entomologists also talk about "true bugs," which are a special group of about eighty thousand species of insects with sharp, sucking mouthparts that form a "proboscis" or beak. Most true bugs are vegetarians. They suck the sap out of plants, sometimes causing great harm to crops. But some true bug species have a taste for blood—usually the blood of other insects.

Ambush bugs are true bugs and ferocious predators with mantislike front legs. Their greenish-yellow color makes them hard to see on goldenrod, a common yellow wildflower that grows along roadsides and in fields. Some ambush bug species are helpful to humans, ridding fields of pests. Others kill beneficial insects like bees. Sometimes they eat each other: even an ambush bug can be ambushed!

HERE
I AM!

To my cousin, Susan Sholin, with uncamouflaged affection.—D. S.

To my parents, Stu and Ethel, in honor of their 60th wedding anniversary!—Y. S.

To my special granddaughter, Meghan.—D. K.

TRICYCLE PRESS

an imprint of Ten Speed Press

PO Box 7123, Berkeley, California 94707

www.tricyclepress.com

Design by Melissa Brown except for the ambush bug poem on page 46, which was designed by Melissa Brown and Katy Brown

Typeset in Grilled Cheese and Lisboa

Library of Congress Cataloging-in-Publication Data

Schwartz, David M.

Where else in the wild? / by David Schwartz and Yael Schy ; eye-tricking photographs by Dwight Kuhn.

p. cm.

Includes bibliographical references and index.

ISBN-13: 978-1-58246-283-7 (hardcover : alk. paper)

ISBN-10: 1-58246-283-6 (hardcover : alk. paper)

1. Animals—Juvenile literature. 2. Camouflage (Biology)--Juvenile literature. I. Schy, Yael. II. Kuhn, Dwight, ill. III. Title.

QL49.S2752 2009

2008042430

First Tricycle Press printing, 2009

Printed in China

1 2 3 4 5 6 — 13 12 11 10 09